Thumb Position Duets for the Cello

Book One

by Cassia Harvey

CHP144

©2018 C. Harvey Publications® All Rights Reserved.

www.charveypublications.com - print books

www.learnstrings.com - PDF downloadable books and chamber music

Allegretto

Campagnoli, arr. Harvey

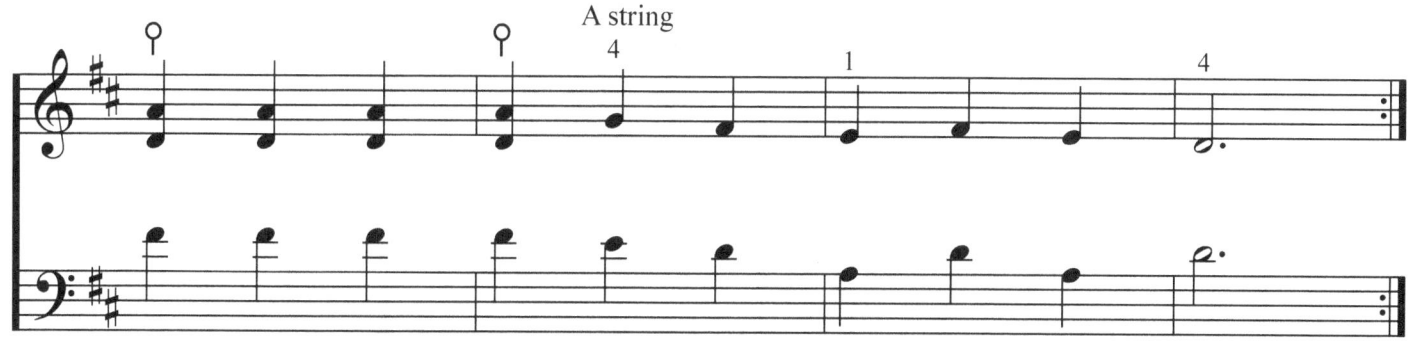

©2007 C. Harvey Publications All Rights Reserved.

Repetition

Breslauer, arr. Harvey

©2007 C. Harvey Publications All Rights Reserved.

Allegretto

Cramer, arr. Harvey

Down in the Valley

Traditional, arr. Harvey

Sonata

Mozart, arr. Harvey

Andante

Cramer, arr. Harvey

The Blacksmith

Traditional, arr. Harvey

Fantasia

L. Mozart, arr. Harvey

Thumb Position Duets for the Cello, Book One

11

Allegretto

Le Couppey, arr. Harvey

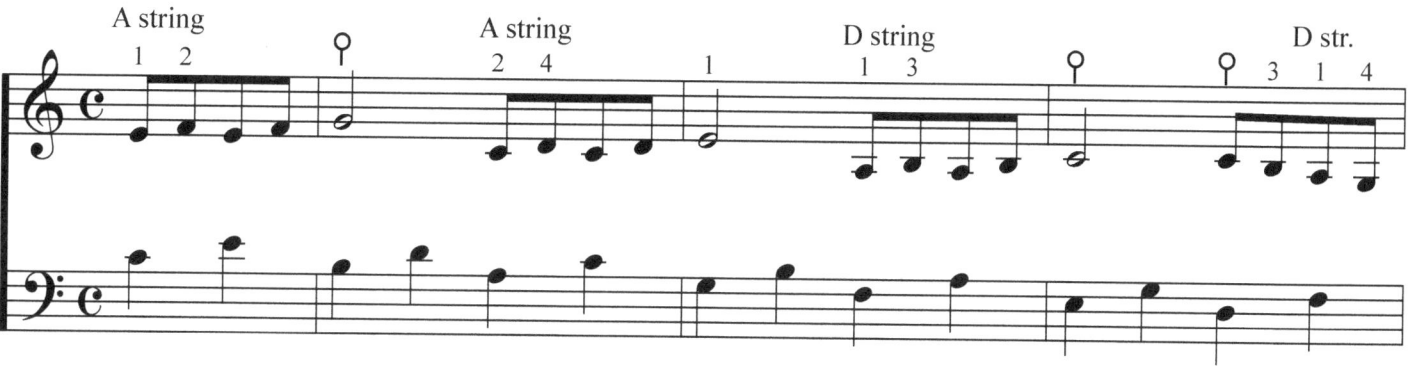

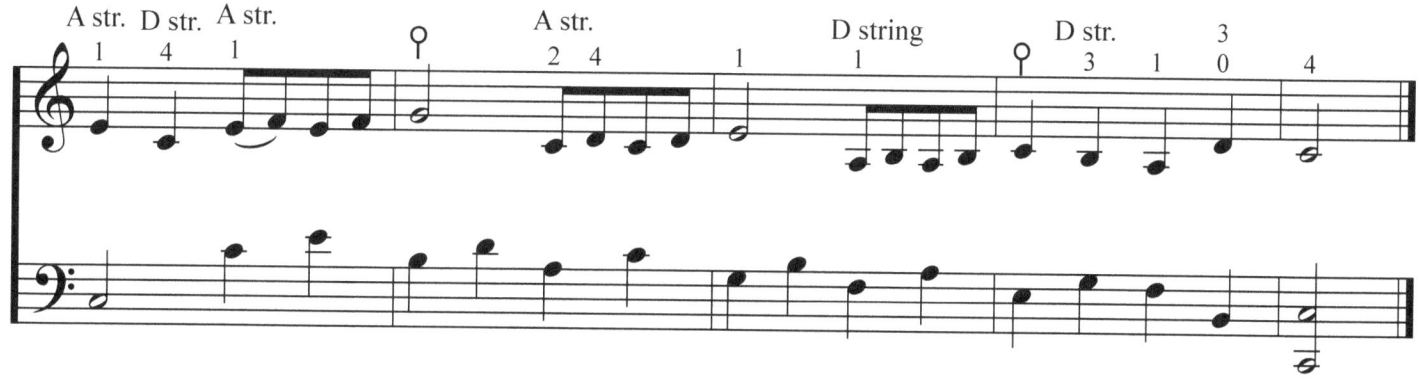

Etude #17

Lee, arr. Harvey

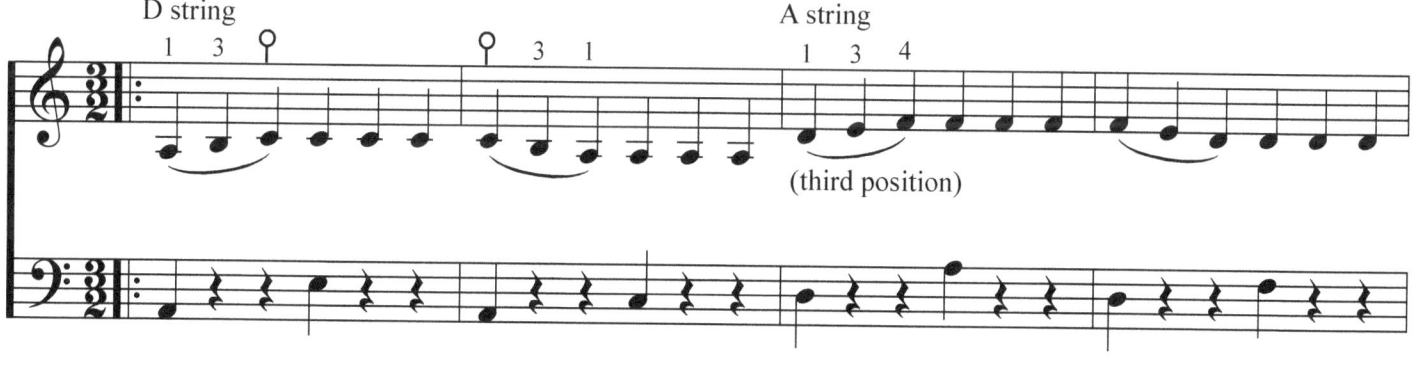

©2007 C. Harvey Publications All Rights Reserved.

Concerto

Schroetter, arr. Harvey

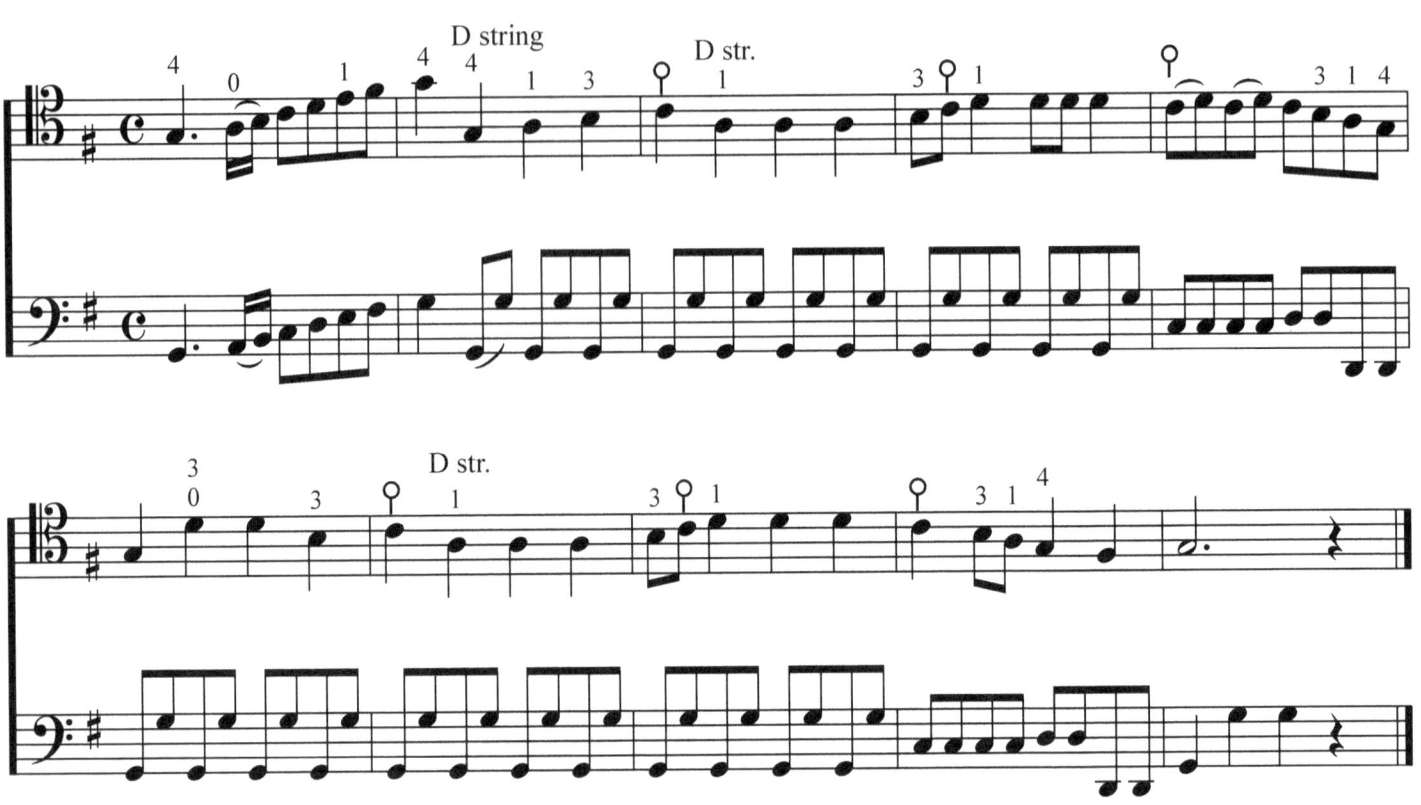

Camptown Races

Foster, arr. Harvey

©2007 C. Harvey Publications All Rights Reserved.

Brother and Sister

Breslauer, arr. Harvey

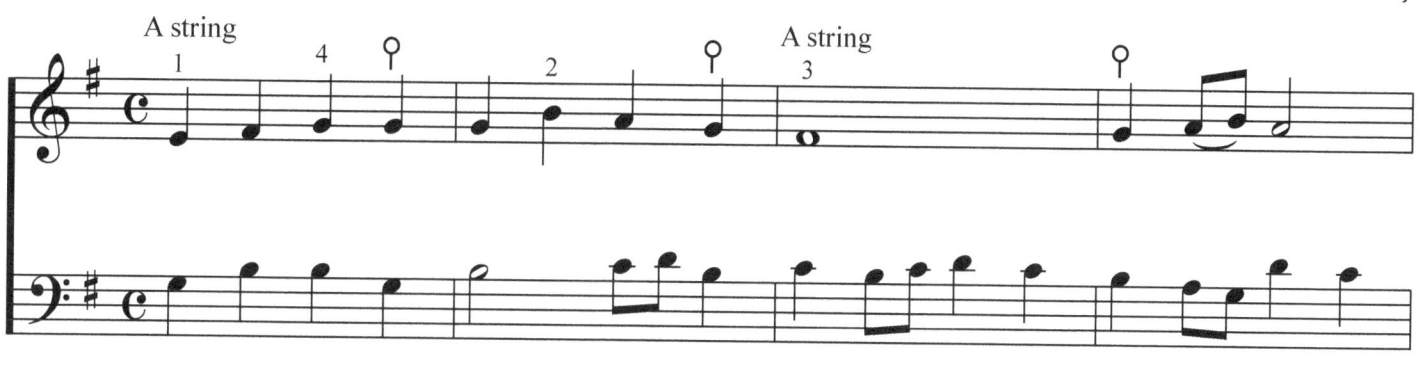

Suo-Gan

Traditional, arr. Harvey

Dance

C. Harvey

Sonata

Somis, arr. Harvey

©2007 C. Harvey Publications All Rights Reserved.

Reel

Traditional, arr. Harvey

Aria I

Schall, arr. Harvey

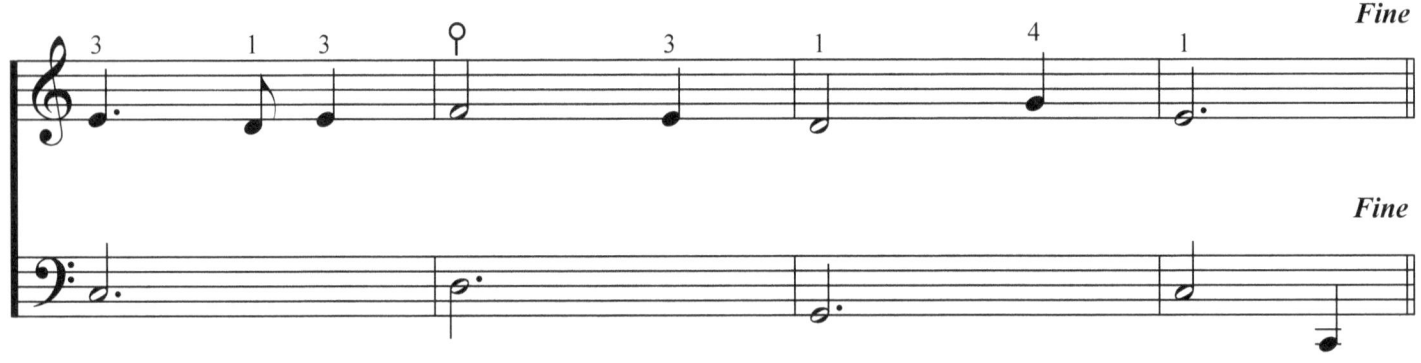

©2007 C. Harvey Publications All Rights Reserved.

Mountain Ash

C. Harvey

The Peacock and the Hen

Traditional, arr. Harvey

©2007 C. Harvey Publications All Rights Reserved.

Praeludium

Heller, arr. Harvey

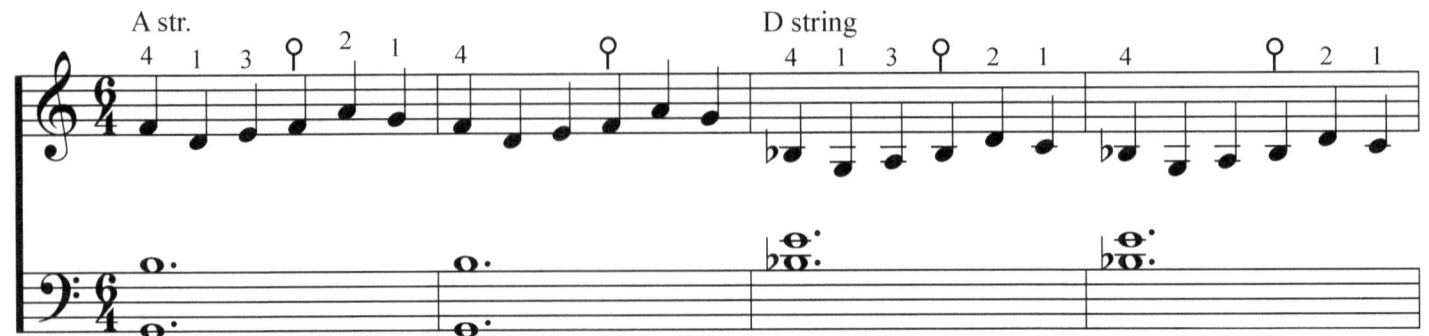

Fiddle Tune

C. Harvey

©2007 C. Harvey Publications All Rights Reserved.

Allegro

Thumb Position Duets for the Cello, Book One
Valentini, arr. Harvey

©2007 C. Harvey Publications All Rights Reserved.

The Young Widow

Traditional, arr. Harvey

Theme

Weber, arr. Harvey

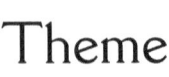

Contredanz

Thumb Position Duets for the Cello, Book One

Bast, arr. Harvey

Emperor of the Moon

Playford, arr. Harvey

Quadrille

Traditional, arr. Harvey

Mount Hills

Playford, arr. Harvey

©2007 C. Harvey Publications All Rights Reserved.

Minuet

Bach, arr. Harvey

March

Bach, arr. Harvey

©2007 C. Harvey Publications All Rights Reserved.

Menuet

Bast, arr. Harvey

©2007 C. Harvey Publications All Rights Reserved.

Thumb Position Duets for the Cello, Book One

Allegro in Different Keys

C. Harvey

Thumb Position Duets for the Cello, Book One

33

©2007 C. Harvey Publications All Rights Reserved.

available from www.charveypublications.com: CHP261

Thumb Position School for Cello

Thumb Position in D Major

Cassia Harvey

Intonation Study

Finger Exercise

©2015 C. Harvey Publications All Rights Reserved.

www.ingramcontent.com/pod-product-compliance
Lightning Source LLC
Chambersburg PA
CBHW051428070526
44584CB00023B/3626